Dear Monica,

FROM
CHAOS
TO
CALM

How to create and maintain a perfectly run household

Such a pleasure! Enjoy the read,

MARTIN HIGGINS

WOW Book Publishing™

Warmest Regards, Martin

First Edition Published by Martin Higgins

Copyright ©2019 Martin Higgins

WOW Book Publishing™

ISBN: 9781074012427

Dedication

I dedicate this book to employers and employees in the Domestic Service Industry.

I hope that in reading this book, you can benefit from my many years of experience and learn the easy way to enjoy your harmonious household.

It is my aim to be able to give back to this wonderful profession that has given me so many years of happiness and success.

A 'How to' book for new or existing employers of domestic staff, to source the best staff on the market for your needs and how to effectively run your home.

Contents

Acknowledgement

Iacknowledge all of the wonderful employers I have had the immense pleasure of working for over my career and for giving me the information and skill set to be able to compile this book.

I also acknowledge the many dedicated staff and service providers I have had the honour to work with.

I acknowledge my dear friends, Lady Cromer and Award Winning Author Vishal Morjaria, as well as my family and supporters of this book for their help in the process of writing and creating it.

I also acknowledge Sunday Times Best Selling Author and Professional Speaker Andy Harrington for inspiring me to follow my passion.

Finally, I acknowledge you for receiving this book and for using it in the most positive way that you know.

Testimonials

'You know just what to do and how to do it.'—International UHNW client, Manhattan

'What would we do without you? Your work is beyond reproach: always thoughtful, elegant and highly professional' —International UHNW client, Manhattan

'We depend on your leadership and advice more and more and seem to need you more and more . . . '—UHNW client

'So thrilled to have you supervising our homes, no one has your magic nor your touch. You are a dear man and an angel' —UHNW client

'Your support has helped the efficiency of our home and lives; we share more precious family moments together as a consequence. Thank you!'—Family Household, North London

'Thank you once again for helping make our lives so pleasant.' —UHNW client, Fifth Avenue, Manhattan

'Thank you so much for looking after us again so well'—Ducal Household, Hyde Park Corner

Foreword

Dear Reader,

From Chaos to Calm, is THE book you need to read and learn about in order to be able to have a wonderfully run home.

Martin has acquired some masterful skills and knowledge and he imparts it to you in a way that will allow you to understand and apply it immediately.

The knowledge in this book has the power to help you create the organised household you desire.

I only wish Martin had written this book sooner, so I would have benefited from his wisdom in putting together my household.

Martin has the expertise, skills, spirit and heart necessary to help you with any household organisation issue you may have.

—Shelley Hu,
The Countess of Cromer

Preface

Are you an employer of domestic staff and have experienced a high staff turnover in your household or are afraid of losing good staff? Maybe you have had bad experiences in finding replacement staff over and over again? Perhaps you are considering employing home help and don't know the 'ins and outs' of the business? If so, then this book is for you!

I have worked in some of the most well run homes around the world and had the honour of working for some wonderful families for whom I have sourced exceptional staff who remained faithful to them for many years.

In this book, I will lay out strategies and key points, along with some valuable pieces of knowledge I have acquired over my 30 years of experience working in some of the most discerning residences worldwide. Whether you are looking to replace a key member of staff or are looking to find a daily cleaner for a pied-a-terre, the principles are the same.

Let me share with you my knowledge and experience so you too can find the BEST staff for your needs who will want to stay looking after you for many years to come.

It is my dream to pass on all I have learnt over the years. I understand and have experienced so many problems that exist in households, and I am passionate about offering sound advice and easy-to-follow solutions so that you can overcome many of the obstacles you may be facing right now.

So many times, I have heard the same issues from my clients and staff alike, which can be boiled down to one very simple solution.

Come with me now, and let me put you on the path to having a wonderfully run and harmonious home!

Prologue

As most employers of domestic staff know, it is hard to find good people, and sometimes, even harder to keep them. Whether it is a daily cleaner, or a full household of professional staff, the problems are the same.

Using an agency usually involves high fees, which may well be warranted—if they do a good job—but if the staff leaves after the guarantee period expires (normally 3 months), then you are back to square one, with any fees and time spent on training lost.

If you decide to use online recruitment sites, then you will likely spend so much time on reviewing CVs, making telephone calls, reference checks and interviewing, which can devour most of your valuable time.

Finding candidates through friends, or friends of existing staff, i.e. by word-of-mouth or referrals, can be a good strategy but unfortunately not foolproof. There are so many factors that could lead to a bad 'match'—i.e. different set of duties, clashes in personality, working hours, location, and so on and so forth.

I will be providing you with detailed information that will work year after year.

So, what is this strategy, and how will it be useful to you?

In my 30 years of experience in working and running some of the top households around the world, I have had the good fortune to work with some of the finest staff, with incredible attitudes and some of the most wonderful employers. However, I have also worked with less exemplary staff and employers who, for whatever reason and in whatever way, did not provide a positive working environment.

In the chapters that follow, I will aim to break down my strategy into easy-to-read chunks that you can follow and adopt so that you can create your own harmonious and well run household that your friends will envy!

CHAPTER 1

About the Author

My name is Martin Higgins. I grew up in Solihull, West Midlands, England.

I knew at a very early age, when I was seven I think that I wanted to be a butler and work in beautifully appointed homes creating an atmosphere of calm and elegance. Whether this was from my passion of English Stately Homes and architecture, or my love of the hit series of the time, 'Upstairs, Downstairs,' I just knew that that was where my vocation lay.

For that, I have always been so grateful, as I have been able to steer my career from such an early age, giving me perhaps a head start over my peer group, who may not have known their true career path until much later, or indeed even now.

My parents, sister and I moved into a rather lovely 1930s four-bedroom detached suburban home shortly after I was born until I was 13 years old. It was a house which we all loved very much.

From such an early age, I started running it as if I were the butler, constantly cleaning, tidying, polishing the silver and laying the dining room for what would appear to be multi-course banquets, when indeed we were only having egg and chips!

To this day, I was never sure if my parents were humouring me or if they simply enjoyed the experience!

The house was often on the market as my parents were keen to purchase a new property. We finally achieved the sale, but for many years we would have the 'FOR SALE' board up outside and several times a week, the doorbell would ring, and there could stand the potential next owner.

Anxious to make the best impression, I would whiz round, moving from room to room before they were shown through, straightening the furniture and the beds, plumping the cushions, tidying surfaces with such haste as to ensure the moment the viewers were shown to the next room, it would be perfect. I would do this time and time again, refining my technique –great training for my potential career! Our efforts paid off, and we moved to a new house in 1985.

This was now a new experience. I loved interior design and gardening, so this provided a blank canvass on which I could work.

My father and I planned and laid out the garden, whilst I also gave my opinion on the interior design; for which my parents were always so very accepting, and amazingly quite happy to give me pretty much a free reign. I loved planning the layout of how best furniture, lighting and ornament should be placed, and learning the importance of detail.

At the age of twelve, I didn't think that a career as a butler existed in early 80s Britain, so I decided that a career in

Hotel Management would be the closest to that of domestic service. I also had a passion for The 'Ritz' in London. So, from completing my 'O' levels, I put myself through Hotel School and had an extensive education in Hospitality and Hotel Management, whilst working part-time in local hotel kitchens and restaurants.

My first part-time position was at a small local hotel, where I began a Saturday job in the pot wash. Within the year, I was running the kitchen when the chefs were off.

I will always remember a piece of advice the Hotel Manager told me at the time—the most important job in the hotel was that of the pot wash, mainly because, if for whatever reason the pot wash wasn't there, as it is the only job that nobody else wants to cover, but a job that, although on the bottom rung of the 'job chain,' if the pots and dishes weren't getting washed and put back properly, it would disrupt the whole process of service.

This gave me an appreciation and respect for that position. So from then on, I have never considered any role beneath me and respected every staff member in whatever position they are in.

You should not expect staff to respect you,
if you cannot respect them.

After four years of studying and working in various other hospitality positions, I graduated from Catering College. I had, by this time, been working at a local hotel restaurant as a waiter. The General Manager was planning to relocate and open a brand new 5-Star hotel, destined to be the flagship of the group. The finest hotel in The Midlands. My level of service and attitude must have been noted, as he invited me to join his management team.

I began as the Assistant Food and Beverage Manager, working alongside the Assistant 'F and B' Manager—a great partnership. We were involved with the initial hiring procedure, then when our full team was in place, I created the standards of performance manuals for all the F and B departments; set up the wine cellar; and scheduled all the deliveries—from carpets, furniture, linens and china to ordering and receiving the wines and spirits and so on and so forth. We practically worked around the clock, but had such pride when the hotel opened as our reviews and standards were first class.

Sadly, the GM turned out not to be someone who possessed the character and disposition I originally thought. From a figure I initially looked up to and was proud to work under, I began to realise he had many flaws, not least his violent temper and unpredictability. Consequently, he lost almost his entire management team, and relied on the two of us to not only oversee the F and B departments and control the cellar requisitions on a daily basis, but for a month or more cover 24-hour Duty Management shifts.

At this time, I was often reprimanded, many times in front of others, for not being 'Front of House' and available to our guests. Being so short staffed, I thought my priorities lay in ensuring the back of house operations were carried out so each department had the stock required to function. I look back now, and thank him for his behaviour. As he instilled a sense of urgency in me, and the knowledge that it did not matter how many staff we were short on, or what was going on or not going on behind the scenes. The level of service and visibility was paramount.

The guest should never be compromised
no matter what.

I have never forgotten this important nugget of information in my education. Nor have I forgotten his behaviour and treatment of his team. Shouting and screaming at, not only I, but all key employees who only wanted to learn and please. His behaviour accomplished nothing; the negative energy he created only caused resentment and nervousness, which is never a good environment to be in, least of all to work and give your best.

It was at this time, I noticed a position advertised as:

'Under Butler wanted within The Royal Household,
Buckingham Palace.'

After realising that my vocation did indeed lie in private service, I applied, and was accepted for an interview, and within two weeks, took the position within The Royal Household. It was quite a surreal moment for me, as I was entering a mystical world I had only previously dreamt of.

I was employed at Buckingham Palace as a footman and under butler for over 3 years—a prestigious start to my career in the private service industry.

I was part of a wonderful team of young butlers responsible for the storage, cleaning and organisation of the silver and gilt at Buckingham Palace. I have always loved silver, so for me, this was a dream come true!

I thoroughly enjoyed the task of cleaning some incredible pieces of silver, often spending days on one item meticulously removing years of built up polish from the intricate flourishes, garlands and figures decorating beautifully ornate salvers, teapots, epergnes and other priceless tableware, with soft brushes, toothpicks and cotton buds!

We were also charged with setting the table for all Royal meals, from daily lunches and dinners to the formal State Banquets. It would take about a week to set the table for a State Banquet; from selecting the items to be used, to cleaning them, bringing them to the table and placing each piece to the millimetre so as once complete, every single item on the table would be perfectly in line—quite a sight to behold.

Of course, if the items, especially each place setting, were not measured, then not only would the table look unsightly, (especially being OCD!) but once you arrived at the end of the table you may either run out of place settings or run out of table, and spend the next millennia shuffling everything back and forth to fit!

After over 3 years having served a glittering ensemble of celebrities, Heads of State, Presidents and some of the most important figures of the day, and worked with the finest silver, gilt, porcelain and crystal amidst rooms filled with priceless art furniture and ornament. The legacy I have been given is that I am no longer fazed or star struck when introduced to, or upon opening the door to any public figure, and can now handle, look after and respect the finest and most delicate of tableware and antiques.

One afternoon, I received an anonymous phone call from a rather well-spoken lady, who told me ' . . . I know you, but you don't' know me!' I was intrigued! I went out to meet her there and then, and it turned out that she was a top staffing agent in London and wanted to offer me a position.

The position was Chief Steward aboard a 54-metre private yacht in the Mediterranean—how could I resist! I accepted the position and spent the next year with a truly lovely Italian Doges family cruising the Med. It was World Cup year too, and Italy made it to the Semi Finals!

The standards onboard were meticulously high. To give an example, many of the interior walls were suede, upholstery velvet and all the carpets showed footprints. Consequently, I was constantly brushing the suede and velvet and jumping between the oriental rugs to avoid showing footprints on the carpet. I even carried around a comb to straighten the fringes on the rugs. So, after the family and guests had departed after two weeks or more of being onboard, I had to literally make 'snow angels' on the carpet, mess up the fringes, the velvet and suede for my own sanity!

This was my first position working in a 100% heterosexual environment. My fondest memory was the weekly wash down (of the boat!); when the crew were all out on deck cleaning the paintwork to remove the salt water.

As I was in charge of the Interior, I controlled the music . . . consequently, whereas most of the yachts had R&B and more mainstream music, we had everything from Shirley Bassey, disco and show tunes blaring out across the marina! The crew seemed to love it; they danced and camped it up and got the work done in no time. The Captain allowed it, but was however, a little less complimentary—probably embarrassed! I hope from that, he realised that a fun working environment connected us all and how important it is to have light hearted even silly moments, even in the most formal of environments to blow off steam.

I was 25, and now 25 years later, it seems hard to believe that I was having a midlife crisis! I needed to make some roots. I contacted the 'well-spoken lady' and she found me a new role . . .

I returned to the UK and worked as second butler for a financier and his family; based in a delightful town in Berkshire.

The family owned several large residences around the world, and there was a team of four of us who travelled between them as their 'core' crew, the butler, second butler, chef and lady's maid. We worked very well together, complimenting each other wonderfully. We ensured the family's wellbeing at all times. From our close dealings with one another, I understood the importance of precise communication and unity in this close knit group, as we relied on each other to pass on key information and complete tasks for one another to be able to work effectively and efficiently as a whole to ensure that each of us had the support we needed.

After New Year, the family would head to their five-storey residence in the Swiss Alps, where they would stay for several months. During this time, they entertained significantly and had glamorous weekend house parties from Thursday through Monday week after week for around 15 plus guests. Consequently, I was up by 6am cleaning out and relaying five fireplaces before serving a full breakfast, then assisting housekeeping with completing the bedrooms. There would generally be a couple of guests who didn't ski to whom we served lunch, then we prepared for a cocktail party and dinner, often finishing in the early hours. We had fun along the way and managed to enjoy the resort.

I recall one instance, where the butler locked me in the chocolate room as a prank! (Yes! There was a room dedicated to chocolate—it was Switzerland after all!) I thought, 'to hell with this, I'm going to eat some chocolate'...and in the pitch darkness, selected what I thought was an orange cream. Unfortunately, it was a chocolate covered Brazil nut, and I had a nut allergy! In the darkness, it took several moments to realize my mistake, enough time however, to digest the rogue legume!

When I was finally allowed out, the look of horror on the butlers face was such that after ingesting all the milk, yoghurt and cheese I could find, to help reduce the irritation, I realized I had to race back to my villa, where I took an antihistamine. The projectile vomit that followed was legendary! I was back to normal in an hour, just enough time though to miss dinner service and ensure the butler handled it on his own - a fair cop I thought!!!

It was long hours over several months which, even though I adored the family and my colleagues, wore me down and I realised I could not carry on in this situation for much longer.

I now know how important both effective communication and appropriate working standards are, as I didn't complain nor moan at the workload, but in trying to be an exemplary employee, I took it on the chin until I became overloaded and ready to leave, thus causing the family and staff further problems in replacing me. Since then, further staff were employed, and the family vacated for two weeks thus allowing the staff a two-week vacation in Switzerland half way through their trip. If I had been open and discussed my situation, I may well be still working for them to this day.

I had good friends who ran a prominent London staffing agency, who, in retrospect, had a rather difficult client who was in need of a butler. I wanted to be based in London, but this client was on 5th Avenue in Manhattan. I had never been to New York, which coincidently was high up on my list of places to visit. The temptation was high! I was to meet the client in Paris, as she was on a shopping trip in Europe locating furniture for a new residence.

We met in the lobby of the Ritz in Paris, and if I was to undertake this role, it was going to be a life changing position. Consequently, I was the one who interviewed her –asking all the most pertinent questions to obtain a full perspective of what I would be letting myself in for. She knew very well at that moment that I was taking this seriously and consequently our rapport was excellent and after less than an hour, she offered me the position there and then. Bearing in mind, as I found out later, she had employed eleven butlers who did not work out in the same amount of months.

The Interview is such an important part of the engagement process. The interviewer should already know, from the CV (points that we can go through later in this book), having already ascertained what their requirements are, that the interviewee can fulfil those needs. The interview stage is all about rapport. I can tell within three seconds of meeting if a candidate will be successful or not. We will discuss these points of reference later on.

I took the bold step and uprooted once more and moved to NYC. It was an incredible time, and enjoyed it very much, though it certainly had its ups and downs.

I was to run an exceptional apartment, both in size and design, on 5th Avenue, almost opposite The Metropolitan Museum on 'Museum Mile'. The views on all sides were just beautiful and the Main Reception Rooms overlooked Central Park.

I learnt a tremendous amount during my years in that position, both from my employer and from being a member of the household. There were five other members of staff that were based in the New York apartment and I was the head of the team. My relationship with my employer was great; we had a mutual respect and I admired her greatly. I realized that although she had exceptionally high standards and expected 100% dedication, I offered 110% dedication, and my standards were higher!

Unfortunately, this caused some jealousy among the other staff, who I now understand were put out when I appeared and increased the Principles expectations, so much so, that at one point, she received an anonymous letter made out of letters cut out of a newspaper (very cliché!) telling her how awful I was and that I should be let go. It was quite a shock, as she showed me the letter and we both had to carry on, knowing that someone in the household sent it. There was a high staff turnover, so I can only assume that whoever sent it left shortly afterwards. I was young and eager to please, and wanted to ensure a perfect environment for my Principle, which put a strain on the other staff members, who probably had an easier time prior to my arrival.

I understand the importance of creating a cohesive team – a team that can communicate and understand one another. I learnt the hard way, so from experience, the need to nurture and understand everyone's point of view, situation and even body language is crucial. Many times, people keep their true emotions hidden, and if this is a negative emotion and is not addressed, at some point it will come out in really distressing ways. We were dealing with crisis situations and staff problems left and right. Sometimes, it is down to the employer, or their representative, to look at the bigger picture and understand the point of view of a staff member who is not performing well. There can be so many reasons that may not be of their doing, but something that has been irking them over time and that they have not felt secure enough to bring it up.

I stayed in this position for 10 years, working and overseeing the family's other estates around the US.

In 2001, my partner of five years became very ill. He was HIV positive and his immune system had practically given up.

He was a flight attendant for a major US airline and flew long haul on a weekly basis. It was the morning of September 11, and he was due to fly to London that evening. Needless to say, on that fateful day, he did not fly, but witnessed the attack on the World Trade Centre from our apartment. He went into hospital a few days later, and became increasingly worse. It really was an awful time, but the spirit that existed in New York at that time, can be best described as the spirit of The Blitz in London during the Second World War. So many New Yorkers, normally perceived as brash and uncaring, became the most caring and generous. It was quite a surreal time to be there.

My partner, Jeff, went in and out of various hospitals for the next few months, and his health deteriorated. My employer knew what the situation was. She told me to do whatever I needed to and not to worry about anything else. She used her connections to admit him to the best hospital and ensure he received the finest care. For this, I am forever in her debt. He lost the power to communicate in the last few months of his life, so I was living next to his bedside in hospital as his eyes and ears. He passed away in the early hours of Valentine's Day surrounded by his family and friends. To this day, I am so grateful that I was the one chosen to be there for him.

I stayed in New York for another few years. I had trained the staff and set up the households so they were able to run with less and less input from me. I had almost made myself out of a job. I was missing my family, and knew, in my heart of hearts, it was time to return to London.

In the spring of 2005, I returned to London and desired a change in career. With this in mind, a friend and I co-created an online domestic staff recruitment site, the first of its kind.

We knew there was a gap in the market, as although there were some fantastic agents for domestic staff, there were also many unscrupulous ones. Other than placing an advertisement, or responding to an advertisement in various related publications or through word-of-mouth, there was no other way to find good staff. We understood the issues that both employers and candidates had, and we wanted to somehow 'give back' to the industry, and provide a forum where employers and employees could easily connect without the need of a third party and expensive fees via a search facility. This way, they could chat online and arrange an interview if appropriate.

In 2006, I turned my efforts to run and manage the various households worldwide of a HNW family. Based in Belgravia, I oversaw the staffing and installation of various new estates ranging from one of the larger apartments on Eaton Square, two of the finest apartments in Manhattan, a Palladian mansion in Malibu, and magnificent estates in Majorca and Beverly Hills.

Through my professionalism, reliability, diplomacy and extensive experience in all fields of private service, they trusted me to interview, hire, train and supervise staff, manage the estate's administration as well as manage the daily running of their multiple residences on a 'hands-on' basis.

Combining my years of experience with my empathetic and compassionate nature, I find I can work easily with both employers and staff alike to discuss areas that require help, and thus work effectively and joyfully with staff to train and bring them up to scratch. I know the importance of harmony in a household and how strong organisation and communication is vital to the smooth running of any home.

I understand too, how important it is to have synchronicity between a family's various residences and a communication network that allows one to access key information at a moment's notice, without the issue of different time zones.

Now, I am based in London, and have turned the talents and experience of the last 30 years to the creation of House Martin of London in handling all aspects of effective household organisation.

During this time, I have witnessed many of the same pitfalls and problems that exist in almost every household. In my efforts to provide a service that could be beneficial to the smooth organisation and seamless service, we have created a software application that we can apply to any household environment to address these problems and pitfalls. But more about that later. . . .

CHAPTER 2

How I can help you?
The Strategy from Chaos
to Calm

I hope this book will lead you through the steps on how to engage the right staff for your home and the ways in which to keep them motivated and run your home impeccably!

To have the confidence and assurance that your home or homes are in the hands of people you can trust so you can concentrate on your life and business is what dreams are made of. It is obtainable! However, getting to that point can be akin to climbing a mountain and for some, the flag is never pitched on the peak; they keep returning to base camp to try, try and try again, but coming back less motivated each and every time.

However, imagine returning home, or arriving at one of your residences that you may not have visited for months, and you drive through the gates, all the driveway lights work, the grounds are manicured, and on reaching the front door, your staff greet you with a smile, take your bags and on entering the hall, fresh flowers and the scent of your favourite candle welcome you.

Dinner awaits you, and while you dine on your favourite dishes cooked perfectly, there is no noise coming from the kitchen, your glasses are kept filled, and on heading to bed, your luggage is unpacked and everything steamed and neatly put away in its correct place, the bed turned down and the lighting levels and temperature set perfectly. You can sleep well!

However, as we know, many times this is sadly far from the case! Many employers of domestic staff know it is a constant problem to find good people, and sometimes, an even bigger problem to keep them. Also, the employment process is nothing but a vortex of time and money. Not to mention the time in getting to know and like them, to train them to your standards and requirements and to finally get to a point of trust.

It can be your worst nightmare when a trusted member of staff comes to you and asks for their resignation. Your worst nightmare has come true; visions of countless housekeepers at your door, dressed as Mary Poppins waiting for you to interview them fills your mind with dread! You just wish for that gust of wind to blow away all but one who will magically transform your home into a haven of harmony and domestic bliss! Well, I want to be that gust of fresh air for you!

So, in true Disney fashion, let's turn the page and begin!

Where do you start?

You really have three alternatives to finding domestic staff. These are:

1.   A Domestic Staffing Agency

2.   An On-line Database

3.   Word of Mouth

What would constitute a positive working environment?

It is one that enables motivated staff to work efficiently and harmoniously as a team, to complete all the tasks effectively and in a timely manner.

How do I create this 'Shangri La' environment?

You need to provide the following:

•   The right staff for your needs;

•   Effective paths of communication and clear instruction;

•   Promoting comradery amongst staff—through trust, motivation, respect, empathy and compassion;

•   Provide the right equipment/tools for the job;

•   Provide good working conditions.

Carefully consider staff working hours that would accommodate your needs but also theirs, and give sufficient breaks and time off.

CHAPTER 3

How This Strategy Came to Fruition

I developed this strategy through not only working for some wonderful employers but also from learning from them and my colleagues. This was either through experience, both good and bad, as an onlooker, or through conversation with other service professionals.

You can learn so much by simply taking the time to have a brief conversation and listen. Showing that you care goes a long way, and will come back to you tenfold. Empathy and compassion will always win over aggression and negativity.

Who wouldn't want loyal happy staff running their home, as opposed to staff only there for the money, not enjoying their job and giving the minimum effort and respect, or perhaps none at all the moment your back is turned.

My primary role within all these positions was as a diplomat. Having the ability to understand both points of view in most situations has enabled me to rectify and promote harmony in the most difficult scenarios.

I worked for a wonderful employer who I respected tremendously. We understood each other and had similar expectations and standards. Life experiences made her quite distant and untrusting. Sadly, to many, this translated to being cold, hard as steel and incredibly difficult to work for. She had employed eleven butlers in the same amount of months before we met, and staff were in and out of her home like a revolving door. Trying to create a good working environment where the staff were loyal, hard-working, respectful and flexible didn't seem likely.

I needed to turn this around. The day I started, decorators were close to finishing restoring the magnificent reception rooms that had suffered water damage from a major leak from the apartment above us. The housekeeper, who had been there for several years, had lost all motivation, as had most other members of staff, and was performing to the bare minimum, and quite honestly, was not someone who should ever have been employed as a housekeeper in the first place!

She was really nowhere to be found and flatly refused to help put the rooms back once the decorators had left, as it was, in her words ... 'Not my job!' I just did it. No photos had been taken of where the furniture, rugs and objet d'art were to be returned, nor had anything been stored properly, but I had a good idea and did it to the best of my ability. The Principle returned home after a short trip, and was amazed that it had been completed without her having to be involved every step of the way, and that the initiative had been taken. She and I worked together for a short while, just to reposition things slightly, both being OCD. It was a fun experience!

Whilst returning the rooms back to normal, I had made a list of tasks that I noticed needed to be carried out; for example, the newly painted ceilings that now showed up years of dust and soot on the cornice and plasterwork that had not been repainted, furniture that hadn't been waxed for years and so forth. So as well as my other daily duties, I just got on and did it. It took me about two weeks to wash all the cornice on the top of a 12-foot ladder.

The staff reaction was interesting. As I was now in charge, they clearly understood that things were going to change. I made it clear that nobody was to talk about staff behind their back nor speak badly of the employer. I was always smiling and greeting everyone nicely, asking about their work and interests, and even if I knew how best to do something they were doing well, I applauded them and would tell them, I had learnt something from them and thanked them.

The housekeeper left and we employed someone far more suitable. Gradually, other staff members began taking more interest and respect for their work. It was no longer just a job; I had showed that you need to have pride in what you do, and be the best that you can.

After a while, the employer noticed a change in things; that staff were smiling and not complaining every minute. The residence was detailed. Little things (which are ALWAYS the most annoying) such as ornaments put back exactly where they were supposed to, magazines 'lined up', toilet paper always full, toiletries and products magically no longer running out, the fridge stocked and the clocks now always telling the right time and so forth.

She recognised this change, and was consequently less formidable, she smiled to her staff and showed she was pleased and not in the mind-set that they have no respect for her. She began to chat a little, and then at Christmas, everyone received a lovely bonus that showed her appreciation.

The level of work continued to improve, staff stayed and thus employer/staff relationships grew and a level of harmony and organisation prevailed that had never existed before.

**'. . . .lead by example and overreach
your Principle's expectations'**

CHAPTER 4

So, where do you go to find your potential staff?

The 3 alternatives to finding staff

As I mentioned, there are three ways to find staff for your home, and each one has its own merits:

Domestic Staff Agencies—Done FOR you

Online Databases—Done WITH you

Word of Mouth—Done BY you

Domestic Staff Agencies

Domestic Staffing agents have had a bit of a bad reputation recently; some people rely on them completely for their staffing needs, while others avoid them like the plague, preferring to find staff on their own devices. However, using an agent can save you time as they have access to a huge database of possibly all your staffing requirements, and if they are reputable, the staff would already have been vetted, interviewed and criminal record checks carried out before being presented to you. However, like everything else in this world, it comes at a price!

An agent will normally charge anything from 12% to 16% of the candidates' GROSS salary. It will be very important for you to fully understand their terms and conditions before you start working with them.

You should ask any friends or family if they can recommend any agents to you that they have used in the past, and if so, if there is a contact there for you to call.

If this is the case, then you should acknowledge the personal recommendation for several reasons:

1. They know you are serious about finding candidates

2. They will want to give you a great service, so not to endanger an existing client

3. You may be able to negotiate better terms and conditions, such as a lower fee percentage or longer trial period

4. The person that recommended you may be able to receive a 'finder's fee' for recommending to them a new client

As there are many agents, especially in London, you do need to do your due diligence in selecting one. You can of course use multiple agents, and 'hedge your bets'.

How do agents work?

An agent has a large database of trusted candidates in all sectors of household staffing, from private chefs, PAs, butlers, housekeepers and so forth. Some may specialize in certain staff more than others. This is most prevalent with nannies, as you will find many specialist 'Nanny' agencies. They should have background checks, have met or interviewed them (in person, Skype or by phone) and have checked their references and performed background checks. This is a large part of what you pay for, so do make sure you ask that this has been carried out.

You will need to advise them, in AS MUCH DETAIL as you can, what your needs are, who you are looking for, and the conditions of employment—ie location, travel, salary, vacation, hours, other household staff, family members and pets, live in or live out, facilities available (staff room, full laundry) as well as level of experience you require, whether in similar households or otherwise. If you are unsure, then the agent will be able to advise you on any of the above, as they should have years of experience in the industry, and will probably know better than you who you should be looking for. They will then send you their terms and conditions which you MUST review carefully before signing and returning to them.

Once they have your signature, they will begin sending you potential candidates for you to review.

If you are using multiple agents, you MUST be aware that the agent who sends you the successful candidate's name or CV first will achieve the placement.

However, if you decide to only use one agent, you should advise them, and negotiate a lower fee percentage for this. You may want to suggest that you will only use them for a 4 or 6 week period and contact no other agent, and for this, you would like a fee reduction. If after the period has elapsed, and no candidate has been selected, then you will contact other agents.

This will give them a sense of urgency to send you the best candidates to complete quickly.

The agent will communicate with the candidate on your behalf, set up interviews and guide you along the way. Once you have selected a candidate, they will arrange a trial, and can draw up a contract of engagement and advise remuneration and ensure both you and the candidate have everything in place to start the position. They should check in both with you and the candidate in the initial stages of employment, normally within the first few weeks, then send you their invoice which should be paid on time.

If for whatever reason, the candidate proves unsuccessful within the trial period (whatever was agreed upon in the terms and conditions; normally 1–3 months) they will be bound to find you a replacement, or refund your fee, or a percentage thereof, again depending on their terms and conditions.

This is why it is very important to understand the contract before engaging an agent.

I would recommend that a fair contract should read as follows:

10% - 12% fee for being a sole agent

14% - 16% fee for listing with other agents

I would suggest a three month trial period, with a sliding scale of refund (should anything go awry) as follows:

Within the first week a 90% refund

Between weeks 2 and 3 a 60% refund

At week 4 a 50% refund

Between weeks 5 and 6 a 20% refund

It can be a very cut throat industry, and consequently, it does throw up a number of issues you need to be aware of:

- Being bamboozled with too many inappropriate CVs
- Rushed their due diligence to get the CVs to you first
- No thorough reference checks
- Not having met or researched the candidate properly
- Not having reviewed their CVs and references thoroughly, so key details may be missed
- Miss communicated information
- Sending candidates to multiple interviews
- Contacting the candidate once employed to see if they are interested in another position
- Pushing candidates with a history, or withholding details in order to get their fee

Online Databases

Online databases are a fantastic resource to find staff and can be used alongside agents.

However, this does take time, and requires great diligence in selecting suitable staff. You are effectively doing the work of an agent. You will be contacted by many candidates, many of whom will not be suitable for many reasons:

a. Location

b. Experience

c. Salary expectation

Online databases can be a great resource. However, only if you have time and experience in reading CVs and you are happy and confident to make the initial contact and negotiate the terms of employment.

It is important to:

1. Compose a detailed, politically correct job description that contains all the relevant details of both who you are looking for and what the job entails.

    A typical advert may be as follows:

    A First class live-out housekeeper is sought for an UHNW family to join their housekeeping team for a large newly appointed home in Holland Park.

    The successful candidate will need several years experience in working to an exceptional standard, in either private homes or 5-star boutique hotels.

    This will be a fantastic opportunity to work with a wonderful team in an exceptional setting.

    The position will involve taking direction from the lead housekeeper and following checklists to ensure the daily cleaning and periodic deep cleaning throughout the residence is completed to the family's high standards.

    We are ideally looking for a team of 4 housekeepers to ensure that the residence is immaculate, tidy and prepared at all times in accordance with the family's preferences and styling of the home.

The position will also involve helping out the full time laundress when required and assisting with packing and unpacking the family's luggage. As well as working with the Chefs with the cleaning, tidying and washing up in the kitchen.

We are looking to create a harmonious working environment with a 'zen' like feel for both the family and staff alike. A flexible and 'can do' attitude is essential for the role as well as having an attention to detail and being able to take notice of potential issues and reporting them accordingly. A happy and quiet disposition will be a great plus too!

We are more than happy to give ongoing training and support to the right candidate, as we are looking for long-term employees who can grow and be happy working with us for many years to come.

Working hours are based on a 40hr/5 day week. However, we will require the candidate to be flexible and be available to work every other weekend when the family are in residence; with days given off during the week. We are happy to work with the rota as much as we can to accommodate any justified requests and situations, but with the understanding that the family's needs must come first.

**We offer 28 days paid vacation a year, 2 weeks sick pay and an annual gross salary of £??*

2. You need to comprehend your salary level to be able to attract the right calibre of candidates. Therefore, you should look at other adverts and see what the going rate is for the position you hope to fill. Many

applicants do a 'job search' primarily based on the salary and location, so try to fill this in if you can. However, if you are unsure as to what to offer, in your advertisement add 'salary negotiable.' Then on meeting potential candidates, in the second interview, ask them what they were earning in their last position. We will discuss this in more details in a later chapter.

3. Understand employment conditions and what you can and cannot ask for due to PC regulations.

4. You can also review candidates' advertisements and review their CVs and contact them if you think they could be suitable.

5. Work quickly, as time is of the essence, as good staff can disappear quickly.

Word of Mouth/Referrals

Surely engaging staff through a referral from a friend or family member is the best? Well, it can be, but you still need to be diligent about the process as you would by going through an agent or database.

It could make for an entirely different outcome if the employment conditions are markedly different to those where they were previously employed. For example, they may have allowed them to take every Wednesday off to take a driving lesson, and you may need her to drive!

You need to find out key information from your referral before contacting them:

What was the employee's job?

What were their key duties?

How long they were employed for?

Ask for the CV and other references.

What hours and days did they work?

Ask other key questions that are important to you:

For example—were they quiet, detailed, well groomed, etc, etc . . .

Most agents now have an online database that you can access for a fee. You will need to register, and add various details. However, the fee will be significantly less than you would pay to have the process done for you by an agent.

To maximise your net of finding staff, try using a combination of all three options—ask around for both staff that may have just left someone you know or an existing staff knows of anyone who is looking for a position. Anyone they recommend will generally be good, as don't forget, they will be working together and training them to begin with, not to mention that any recommendation will come back to haunt them if it should go wrong!

CHAPTER 5

Who you THINK you NEED Versus whom you REALLY need!

S o, the next step once we have decided on how we will find prospective staff is to determine WHO it is we are actually looking for!

You may have an idea of what you would LIKE. However, this may not necessarily be the right person for you. Many of us would love the idea of a full time butler, catering for our every whim and ensuring our home is organised perfectly, but do you REALLY know what it is that a butler, or indeed other staff members do? As I mentioned in the last chapter, if you engage a reputable agent, they will be able to give you all the direction you need.

However, here is a list of considerations you need to be aware of:

- Do you need someone on a full-time or part-time basis?

- Do you need them to 'live in' or perhaps live locally so they can be available for you quickly?

- Which leads to . . . do you have the room for live-in staff?

A room and bathroom may not be enough? Remember that they do have a life too and will want to come and go, so a separate entrance that will not infringe on the privacy of either party, as neither they nor you will want to be on top of each other. Privacy goes both ways.

If you want to engage a live-in couple for example, the minimum space they will need will be a one bedroom flat or cottage, with a separate bathroom, kitchen, living room and dining area and possibly laundry, and a separate entrance too.

If you have never engaged domestic staff before, you may not have realised that your privacy will now be compromised, whether it be part-time, full-time, live-in or live-out employees.

There are other politically incorrect considerations that people ask about of course, such as age, sex, nationality

and looks, but these are all illegal considerations to make and should not be a consideration in sourcing candidates.

I have listed below some of the key positions, and the main duties and responsibilities associated with each one:

Personal Assistant

A Personal Assistant, or 'PA', must be discrete, discerning and willing to go above and beyond what might be seen as everyday working patterns.

They will be responsible for handling confidential matters, and will take responsibility for scheduling, organizing your calendars for both private and business appointments, arranging public appearances, securing travel arrangements and maintaining itineraries.

The PA may will oversee the household staff and liaise with contractors to arrange for any home maintenance.

To have good chemistry with the personality of their employer is key for a PA. Meeting schedules and the demands of the employer is essential, even if it means doing things normally considered outside the normal scope of the job. Personal assistants bring stability and calmness to their employer's life; even if this means getting their hands dirty or stepping into the shoes of a nanny, housekeeper or chauffeur to fill in the gap!

By nature, PAs must be very flexible, hands-on and capable of multi-tasking to make things happen.

They must work well under pressure, be able to handle hectic work schedules, have high endurance and be willing to work long and odd hours.

Handling correspondence and phone calls, taking care of bills, insurance and other personal affairs, is all included in a PA's duties. They must manage different projects as needed and carry out all necessary research and follow through on personal tasks. They run errands and are often required to shop for gifts and other personal items.

PAs must keep their employers fully abreast of all the day's events to ensure their day runs smoothly. It is a high pressured position which requires efficient systems and software to be in place to be able to co-ordinate everything between the various responsibilities and households effectively.

To assist the PA, and to save time and fine tune their responsibilities, we have created a single, very user friendly software programme that covers many of the tasks a PA carries out. It will allow them to best handle the volume of tasks they need to be on top of, as well as have all the information YOU may need at the touch of a button. It aims to aid the organisation of your various residences anywhere in the world, and give you easy access to your calendars, inventories, manuals or whatever other information you wish 24/7.

We have designed it, so you, the employer, are able to access any information 24 hours a day. Whether it be any one of an infinite number of calendars, from your social calendar to your children's after school activities, or perhaps to view your wine inventory—whether you are on your smart phone, PC or Apple device. You can, for example, check where all your bottles of your Puligny Montrachet are stored. Or you can make a last minute change to your schedule, which can be messaged instantly to your PA or driver or anyone you wish! Consequently, if your PA, or any key member of staff should leave, then all the information will still be very much at hand and easy to access by yourself, the new PA as well as any other pertinent detail required by various other members of staff. We hope that it will allow you to streamline your homes and give you that level of security and peace of mind you deserve! More information is given in Chapter 12!

Butler/House Manager/Major Domo

A Butler, House Manager and Major Domo are very similar roles. The difference will really be determined by the size of your household. In a larger household, the House Manager would be responsible for the smooth running of the residence, with more emphasis on project management, staffing and the various systems in place. The daily running of the residence would be more the jurisdiction of the butler. A Major Domo would be required in a larger, generally more formal home, with jurisdiction over the entire household and multiple residences.

In most staffed homes, the role is combined and will encompass everything from formal table and drinks service, valeting, caring for wines, supervising the other staff members, keeping up morale and ensuring the general upkeep and maintenance of the residence. They would be responsible for the Standards of Performance throughout the home, keeping inventories updated, polishing silver and caring for your fine furniture and antiques.

The butler will be heavily involved with the hiring of your staff. They will need to oversee and manage third party contractors and work with suppliers, as well as assisting you with events and entertaining.

They may be asked to carry out chauffer duties, run errands and even PA duties.

Depending on whom you are looking for, the knowledge and experience of the butler will vary, as you may need someone with a knowledge of guns and experience organising shooting parties, or someone with experience in the kitchen.

The butler would ensure your impeccable standards are maintained, so again there will be a lot of interaction. Consequently, the chemistry between the two of you needs to be very good indeed. They should have a strong eye for detail and a 'can do' attitude.

Typical responsibilities and duties:

- Ensuring the smooth running of a household and servicing of principals and guests, usually supervising others but also providing service
- Engaging and overseeing outside contractors, service providers and suppliers
- Overseeing household staff including hiring, firing, payroll management and performance reviews
- Writing of household manuals and policy documents for owner's approval
- Staff training and development, financial management, budget administration, and purchasing
- Household project management
- Regular maintenance of the property

- Maintaining security and communication systems and record keeping
- Regularly interacting with owners to maintain direct communication and compliance with their needs
- Ensuring efficiency, harmony, and high morale throughout the household
- Organising of social and family events
- Caring for household's guests and visitors
- Serving of wines and other drinks
- Serving of refreshments and meals
- Caring for silver, china, antiques and other specialist items
- Taking on duties of a valet, chef, housekeeper, nanny, pet minder, gardener, or chauffeur if required

The **butler** is a more traditional figure than the **household manager**, and is knowledgeable in etiquette and protocol.

As the position involves a significant level of hands-on service to the owners and their guests, the schedule and hours worked will vary considerably, requiring a large degree of flexibility. Occasionally, such positions are live-in, where security and/or 24/7 on-call services are appropriate.

Qualifications and Skills

- Business and management training
- Certified qualification
- Experience in household and property/project management and residential service

- Vendor and project management skills
- Knowledge of etiquette and protocol
- Experience in formal service of fine wines and food
- Ability to represent the household
- Expertise in caring for fine arts, antiques, silver, china, and cars
- Valeting skills
- Eye for detail
- Ability to anticipate others' wishes and adapt accordingly
- Being discreet, confidential and offering unobtrusive service is de rigeur

Houseman

The role of the houseman is one that is very much hands-on, and ensures the general upkeep of the home. It is a very flexible position that can cover a myriad of tasks depending on the residence. It can cover security, caretaking, gardening and general maintenance and daily cleaning duties, both inside and out.

They may be responsible for keeping the plant rooms and maintenance areas clean and organised, some outdoor work, including car valeting and assisting the interior staff with daily cleaning duties, such as waxing floors, cleaning brasses and changing light bulbs, as well as other handyman tasks. They can also provide extra help during events by assisting with service, setting up and washing up at the end of the night.

Private Chefs

Private Chefs are professionally qualified and will generally have come from a top restaurant or hotel kitchen background. Some may continue attending an academy to improve their skills, or go on stages in top restaurants to keep on top of current trends.

Some chefs will have gained corporate catering experience and most will have experience of varied cuisine, from British, Mediterranean, and French, to Asian, Middle Eastern, Japanese and Fusion.

Often, a private chef will travel with the family between various residences. They will be responsible for food purchases and often provisioning for cleaning materials and drinks, menu planning and preparing and cooking meals, detailing the kitchen and pantries and sometimes serving.

They must know, however, that unlike in a commercial environment, the kitchen remains the property of the family and they should respect your ways and how you want the kitchen organised, and should not rearrange things but always leave the kitchen immaculate ready for you to use.

Attention to detail is also crucial, as is an awareness of food allergies and intolerances with anyone they are serving. Awareness of food safety and hygiene is necessary.

Job roles may extend to assisting with party menu planning, or providing cooking lessons and demonstrations as required. Some may also be required to undertake household management or organise special events. While some private chefs may work as part of a team of household staff, others may work alone or alongside a housekeeper and may be responsible for kitchen budgets and accounts. In larger staffed residences, a personal chef may manage a small team.

Private Chefs are an excellent option for households that require a high standard of cuisine. They can work closely with their employers to cater for specific personal preferences and needs and can cook a range of cuisines catering for specific dietary requirements such as: low calorie, low fat, low sodium, Kosher, Halal, vegetarian, vegan, macrobiotic, diabetic, gluten and dairy free.

Private Chef's salaries are dependent on experience. When selecting a chef, thought must be given to your requirements. They should be aware that they need to cook for staff, nannies and children and provide nutritious meals on a daily basis. Sometimes, if you enjoy fine dining on a regular basis, when eating at home, you may only want comfort food or a simply prepared meal, as opposed to fine cuisine. Consequently, a chef must be happy preparing all manner of dishes and be flexible to your requirements.

Housekeeper/Maid

A good housekeeper provides a wide variety of professional domestic services and can take on all manner of responsibilities as well as cleaning, laundry, wardrobe management, cooking and running errands. Each household has its own particular ways of doing things; therefore, the key duties and responsibilities must be discussed at the interview stage.

Some full-time housekeepers will work on a 'live-in' basis and are provided accommodation and meals in addition to their weekly or monthly salary.

As well as keeping the house clean and orderly, they may also be required to do food shopping and prepare family meals.

It is not uncommon for them to be entrusted with the keys to the household when the employer is not at home. This means they will be able to access the property to work or in the case of an emergency.

Typically, housekeepers will ensure the house is always clean, neat and tidy. They may also undertake some light outdoor duties such putting out rubbish for collection and sweeping terraces and balconies.

It is important that the homeowner's wishes are clear from the outset as housekeeper duties can include:

- Preparing breakfast and cleaning the kitchen and breakfast room
- Keeping the refrigerator clean and discarding out-of-date items
- Cleaning the oven
- Tidying and cleaning bathrooms, bedrooms and living areas
- Cleaning unused rooms on a less frequent basis
- Polishing brass and silver, antiques and fine furniture
- Cleaning windows inside
- Collecting washing, ironing and returning laundry to the appropriate place
- Hand washing delicate items
- Managing the wardrobe

- Arranging dry-cleaning
- Answering the door and telephone
- Feeding and exercising pets on a regular basis
- Keeping patios, pathways and steps clean and tidy
- Watering household plants and flower arranging
- Carrying out weekly grocery shopping
- Handling petty cash and debit cards
- Dealing with tradesmen, suppliers and contractors
- Managing security alarms
- Occasional babysitting
- Carrying out any other tasks that the employer may reasonably ask

Chauffer

Duties and skills of a specialist private chauffeur include:

- Detailed knowledge of local roads without the use of Sat Nav.
- Care and upkeep of all vehicles
- Responsible for ensuring MOTs and car tax is kept current
- Flexibility in taking on duties outside driving such as general maintenance around the employer's home, light gardening and shopping
- School collections and drop-offs for children
- Immaculate presentation at all times, discreet, polite and professional with exceptional time keeping

- Valeting of prestige vehicles
- Opening doors for the clients and guests
- Assisting with luggage

Couples

There are many different variations of couples depending on their abilities, experience and education. For instance, housekeeper/caretaker, cook/handyman, butler/housekeeper, and the list goes on! So again, you need to be crystal clear on what duties you need covered, before commencing the search.

There is always going to be a degree of flexibility in every position and in everyone you engage, but engaging someone in the wrong role can be expensive, especially if two people are involved, for if the position isn't right for one, then you could lose them both.

You also need to understand that, in my experience, very seldom have I met a couple where both parties were equally as strong. Consequently, I recommend that in selecting a couple, you should know what position is more important to be performed, and ensure that that is the role covered by the stronger team member, while the weaker takes the supporting role. There are many dynamics, so don't dismiss the weaker team player, as it could be that their role in the relationship is to allow the other to shine.

Now that I have reviewed some of the various staff roles, I should discuss remuneration . . .

In selecting the right staff, a key component on the quality of personnel you will attract will obviously be how much you are willing to pay!

When deciding upon a salary level for your new staff member, it is very important to ensure that you pay adequately.

This does not mean that you need to pay more than the market value, but that you give value to the services they will perform. A good rule of thumb is to give a rough indication to the agent, if one is engaged, or if selecting candidates from a database state 'salary negotiable based on prior experience'.

Once you interview a prospective candidate, and you reach the final interview stage, you could ask for their previous P60 or P45 so you can see what their previous earnings were. You can discuss with the agent, if one were engaged, and also ask the staff member what their salary requirement is. However, if you do pose this question, ask them to tell you how they came to that figure. Sometimes, candidates don't feel comfortable discussing salary, and defer to their agent.

Remuneration comes in many forms. Sometimes, money is not always the main priority. Working hours, environment, location and so forth may be a deciding factor in them accepting the post. So these areas must also be discussed and factored into the final package. We will talk further on this later in the book on 'providing a good working environment'.

My advice for a full-time staff member would be to offer a starting salary for the first three months, which can be based on the lower end of the salary range discussed. Advise them that after three months, you would like to review their performance (based on their attitude, dedication, attendance record and so forth) and have a general appraisal, and then review their salary accordingly.

Also, as an added bonus, you could give a 'surprise' small lump sum to them at this stage in thanks for their efforts thus far.

An annual salary review, a bonus at Christmas and also for their birthday are wonderful ways to express your appreciation and keep your staff motivated.

September is an excellent time to give an appraisal and pay rise in. Staff would most likely have worked very hard over the summer and would appreciate some positive feedback and gratitude. A good strategy to avert any potential staff losses, as this is an expected time for staff migration, is to give thanks and acknowledge the value of their effort. It is also an excellent opportunity to discuss any issues that may have arisen.

As an employer of domestic staff, you will need to pay your employees' tax, national insurance, and will also be responsible for setting up an employers' pension scheme for all your employees. There are a number of companies that you can engage to set up and manage your payroll— who can also give advice and set up your employers' pension scheme—whether this is for one employee or an entire household.

You will need to agree on whether to pay your employees weekly, bi-weekly or monthly. This will be reflected on their pay slips. All employees on that payroll will need to be paid on the same terms; otherwise, you will need to set up a new payroll, if for example, you agree that one staff member is paid weekly, when everyone else is paid monthly.

You will need to obtain the following details for each new member of staff to send to your payroll provider in order for them to set up their payroll:

Surname

Forename

Current Address

Post Code

Date of Birth

Sex

National Insurance Number

Their Basic Salary

Their standard hours of employment per week

Pay method (ie BACS)

Their Bank Sort Code

Their Bank Account Number

The name of the Bank Account holder

The date their employment starts

If they have an unpaid Student Loan

You will also need to ask them a Starter declaration, to which they can answer yes to either A, B or C:

A. This is my first job since last 6 April and I have not been receiving taxable Job Seeker's Allowance, Employment and Support Allowance, taxable Incapacity Benefit, State or Occupational Pension.

B. This is now my only job but since last 6 April I have had another job, or received taxable Jobseeker's Allowance, Employment and Support Allowance or taxable incapacity Benefit. I do not receive a State or Occupational Pension.

C. As well as my new job, I have another job, or receive a State or Occupational Pension.

You will need to set up direct debits with your bank for your employees' salaries and to HMRC for the collective PAYE and NI contributions, which your Payroll Company will give you in advance.

If you engage freelance staff, normally associated with short-term contracts (i.e. event staff or a temporary butler), they will generally submit an invoice for payment, and therefore will be responsible for paying their own tax and NI contributions.

Now, you need to look at HOW . . .

So, now that you have an understanding of who you need, where to find them and what remuneration to offer, you must look at how to go about selecting them.

Whether you choose to use an agent, online database or have found a great candidate through a friend, the next process will be the same. . . .reviewing CVs.'

CHAPTER 6

How to read a CV. . . .

To be able to read a CV (or resume) is SUCH an important part of the process. Why? Well, this will not only save you an incredible amount of time in interviewing unsuitable staff, but also, expense!

You should always keep an open mind when reading a CV as occasionally, you will come across one that may not contain all the nuggets of information that you have decided qualifies them for the position, but there may be something about it that intrigues you and you should pay attention to that, and arrange an interview regardless. It may be that you come across someone who fits the bill for an entirely different position, or is able to carry out tasks that you may not have even considered!

A CV contains so much information, most of which is not even written. What do I mean?

Well, let's look at the following:

Check for an organised layout

You should be looking for a CV that is ideally two pages or less. Clearly laid out, with plenty of spaces, information neatly lined up in chronological order. It should be laid out so you, the reader, can access the key information quickly and easily. Solid blocks of script, hard to access information and no continuity can mean that the candidate is disorganised and may not possess the order and attention to detail you are looking for.

Review their Photograph

A photograph should always be on the top right hand corner of the C.V. and be about the size of a passport photo.

A photograph tells 1000 words! So, on a CV it can tell you a lot about the candidate. For example, have they attached a passport photo, or an old holiday photo, perhaps of them on the beach, or with friends, and thus not taken the time or effort to take a formal photo –one in which they are well dressed, smart, with a plain or appropriate background, and one in which they are smiling, and thus showing them off in a professional way.

You may want to ask when the photo was taken—it may be 20 years old!

Bad grooming—ask yourself why would they look scruffy in a photo that is representing them for the first time?

However, if a photograph is not on the CV, you cannot ask them to supply one.

Use of language and punctuation

If English is not the candidates' first language and there are numerous grammatical errors, unless the position is for a PA or secretarial post, then you can look past this. I do prefer this as opposed to having the CV written by a professional when it is much harder to 'read between the lines'. I normally allow for two or three mistakes. More than that, then I question the candidates' attention to detail.

Personal overview

It is always interesting reading someone's overview. It tells you a little about their background and what brought them to do what they do, their passions and life experiences that gave them the qualifications and desire to apply for the position with you!

Qualifications

The level of someone's qualifications, other than their intelligence, shows you their ability to apply themselves. A housekeeper from perhaps Eastern Europe, may well have a degree, so combined with a level of relevant experience in various establishments, could indicate their ability to quickly demonstrate management potential. However, just because a candidate may not have the qualifications you are looking for, experience in other areas may very well make up for it.

Work history

You should look carefully as to who they have worked for, the length of service and what their reason for leaving was.

Have they been working for employers on a similar level in society to yourself and with similar standards to your own, in a similar sized residence with a similar sized household and in a similar position to the one they are applying for. If not, you should question their reason for applying.

Have they flitted from positions quite frequently? There may be good reason for this, so if they show promise, you should ask what that reason is, and make sure you check out their references!

If they have worked for only a few employers for long periods of time, you can generally expect that they will consider any new position carefully and only accept if it is something that they know they can handle and enjoy.

You need to question any gaps that may exist between positions. If for any reason, a position did not work out well and they left prematurely or were dismissed, then it may well not appear on the CV, as could a spell at Her Majesty's pleasure.

Hobbies and Interests

It is always a good idea to talk to a potential candidate about their hobbies and interests. It can give you a more rounded opinion of them and you may discover hidden talents!

References and Referees

A CV should ALWAYS be accompanied with a candidate's written references and the contact details for their referees. A referee should ideally be one of their previous employers or a representative who knew them, with whom you can call directly to discuss their credentials should you wish to proceed with their candidacy.

It is illegal to give a bad reference. So you should question why they do not have a reference or a referee from any previous employer. A reference that merely states that they were employed in the position of . . . between the dates of. . . . may require further investigation too.

CHAPTER 7

Interviews, Reference Checks and Trials, Or the '3-Second Rule'!

Interviews

The interview is first and foremost for you to get to know each other and see if the chemistry between you works. Having made it that far, you should know already that they are suitable, and that they are interested in the position. There is no such thing as a bad interview: if you have a good rapport and the interview is enjoyable, then most likely you will move onto the next stage of employment, even if perhaps it isn't for the position you had initially intended. And of course, if there is no rapport, then clearly you will know not to spend further time or money and move on!

Where and when to schedule interviews

An interview for a domestic employee should generally be held at the proposed place of employment, so if it goes well you can introduce them to other staff members and perhaps show them around. However, if you are replacing an employee who is currently engaged, then meeting for a coffee away from the residence is necessary.

You need to be able to give them your complete attention without distractions. This is a very important meeting.

If time is a priority and you are meeting several candidates, and then schedule them together in a morning or afternoon, giving each candidate 30 minutes, with a 15 minute gap between each one.

You need to understand that if a candidate is currently employed, they will only be able to interview on their time off, so flexibility is important. You do not want to employ someone who would happily take a day off sick to attend an interview. The same should apply when offering employment and acknowledging the notice period they need to give. You would want the same consideration in the future.

An initial meeting can be over the phone or on a video call. However, it is never the same impression as meeting in person.

The 3-second rule

This is amazingly accurate! You can generally tell within the first three seconds of meeting an applicant if they will be short listed or not. This actually holds true for meeting anyone. That initial contact on opening the door and seeing them and shaking hands will tell you so much. Whether it is the instant chemistry that may or may not exist between you or any of the following. . . .

1. Facial expression—are they glum or show a nice warm smile?

2. Posture—are they slouching, hands in pockets or standing straight and shoulders back!

3. Do they look smart, well put together or scruffy?

4. Is their choice of clothing and make-up appropriate to the occasion?

5. Are their shoes clean and well-polished?

6. Do they have a good hand shake?

7. Opening words—do they exude confidence and speak clearly?

8. Do they wait to be seated?

Other points to note:

Is their phone switched off, or on vibrate? If it rings, do they answer it and apologise or not?

Do they call you Sir/Madam and show courtesy and respect?

Check their attire, are their nails short and clean? For example, if you interview a housekeeper with long varnished nails and manicured hands, do you really think they are used to deep cleaning, and laundry? Probably not.

Are their shoes appropriate and polished? Wearing shoes that are not polished and in need of some 'tlc' shows a lack of attention to detail and a good indicator of their overall grooming standards.

Do they have a nice confident handshake? Do they smile? Do they wait to ask to be seated?

How is their posture? When they sit, do they slouch or sit neatly not wanting to flatten the cushions? And when they stand, I would give a gold star if they plump up the cushion where they were sitting!

Were they punctual? Sometimes arriving too early is almost as bad as being late.

Do they ask you questions? And if so, are they the wrong questions—ie concentrating on their benefits such as pay, time off, sick pay, as opposed to key elements of what your requirements are?

Ask about gaps in employment, reasons for leaving, what their employers and colleagues were like, if they work well in a team, on their own, ask for examples.

Find out their strengths and weaknesses—ask them: 'So, what are you best at . . . and what areas do you feel you would like to improve? No one is perfect, and in putting together a team, we need to match skills and talents, so what areas do you think you would like to improve upon?'

Ask them what their ambitions are? I.e. where would they like to be in 5 or 10 years' time?

Ask them, what their ideal position would be?

All these questions will get you a better idea as to what their long-term goals are, and if you can nurture them and help them and thus help you. For instance, interviewing a housekeeper who you discover was a book keeper and perhaps has a degree in their home country could, through time and development, be a great candidate for PA.

It is always important to create a good rapport and allow the interviewee to talk. The more opportunity you give them to freely talk about themselves and engage with you, the more poignant details they will divulge. In one interview I held, whilst in conversation with the prospective candidates, it came out that they enjoyed naked sunbathing. I knew that the position for which they were applying allowed them access to the principle's outdoor swimming pool, which was rather overlooked by neighbouring properties. I therefore adapted the House rules to include no staff nudity around the pool. Subsequent staff members have found this rather amusing, as they must have imagined staff being caught running around the estate naked!!

Let them interview you!

Sometimes, the best candidates and the most successful interviews are those that essentially interview the interviewer! It shows that they are serious about the position, they are serious about doing everything to your liking and serious about longevity of service. They are much less likely to move on after a short period of time, as they have amassed all the information they need to make a constructive decision on taking the position or not, should it be offered.

In an interview, if the position they are applying for is for a housekeeper, laundress or butler, or valet, I would ask them if they would be able to iron a shirt. For me, this will show many things about the candidate:

1. Their willingness to carry out the task without questioning.

2. The equipment they normally use, ie a steam iron, or if they can survive using something less sophisticated, should the iron break down during a typical day and they can still perform

3. Their methodology, if they take control and ask where you keep the ironing board, if you have a steam iron, water spray, where you would like them to do it, if they can see the laundry. . . .

4. If they ask you whether you prefer the shirt starched, hung on a hanger or folded—this shows that they are happy to do things your way and do not assume

5. If they remove the collar stays and check the shirt for loose buttons, stains, and so forth prior to ironing—again shows they are detail-oriented

6. If they dampen the shirt first and allow the moisture to penetrate the fibres—normally 15 minutes. If you spray the shirt to dampen it, then iron straight away, the moisture has not penetrated the fabric sufficiently.

7. How they handle the shirt, ie using finger tips in the seams so as not to crease areas already pressed, and the order in which they iron, collar first, then the back, sleeves, front panels and finishing again with the collar, shows they are methodical and know to press the areas not seen first, finishing with the front so as not to make creases through handling nor from pressing other areas of the shirt.

8. How long it takes. Anyone who can press a shirt in under 5 minutes, I would not consider. To press a shirt well, going over areas, checking for creases, ensuring it is done well, it takes around 15—20 minutes.

9. If they fold the shirt, if it is done neatly where the distance from the collar tips to the shoulder is equal both sides, and the splat is centred.

10. If they iron and talk a lot or if they do it in silence is a good indicator of how talkative they will be when employed.

11. If they ask if they can do anything else for you, is a good indicator of their willingness to perform

12. If they tidy up and put away the equipment and not leave it, shows their consideration and that they are tidy and follow through

Reference and CRB (DBS) Checks

I cannot stress enough the importance of reference checking. It can be a tedious task but essential. It is not uncommon for people to embellish their CVs and what they have done and for how long.

The candidate should have contact details for verbal references as well as their written reference letters from their previous employers. It is always a good idea to ask to see the originals, as copies can be 'revised' and adulterated.

Agencies should always check references, but you should always confirm with them that they have!!!

You should always ask the candidate if they are happy that you call their referees. Sometimes, it may be their current employer who may not be aware that they are looking for a new position!

You should really ask for at least three referees.

A referee may be a previous employer, or their PA or an organisation.

When you call, always make sure the person you are speaking to knows the candidate.

Key pieces of information to ascertain:

1. Ask them the 'to' and 'from' dates that they were employed, and check that it corresponds with what they told you.

2. Verify that the place of employment is correct.

3. Ask them what position they held and the duties that they performed.

4. Ask them about their attendance record.

5. Ask them about their attitude and work ethic.

6. Ask them about their overall standards.

7. Ask if they had a good rapport with the Principle and other staff members.

8. Ask them what they were earning.

Ensure you ask pertinent questions relating to the position you want to offer them and ask if they think it would be a good position for them.

Ask the reason why they are no longer engaged.

Most agencies will now also carry out a CRB (Criminal Records Bureau) or DBS (Disclosure and Barring Service) check. It will let you know if the candidate has had any criminal charges made against them. It is a service carried out by a government agency, who you can also contact should you not be using the services of an agent.

The Trial

It is essential that you ask a potential employee to perform a trial BEFORE being offered any position. You need to know that they can actually do the job to the standard you expect, and that you will both get on, and that they will also get on well with any other family household members and staff you may have.

A trial should really be paid for. If after the agreed trial period the candidate proves successful, and they are engaged, then the commencement date of the trial usually becomes the starting date of full employment, and is reflected on their first pay slip. If the candidate is not engaged, then the employer should really pay them for their time, based on the gross daily rate they would have earned.

I would recommend a trial period of 2—3 days, or a maximum of one week. In that time, they should be able to meet the other staff they will be working with, have a tour of the property and work with existing staff members to learn from them and to be encouraged to ask as many questions as they can. Both yourself and they should be able to get a good idea if it will work out during this time.

CHAPTER 8

Engaging your new staff and formulating an Employment Contract

I f you were sourcing the candidate directly, then the only guarantee that you have that they are right for you is in the due diligence you took in going through their CV, references checks, and the candidate completing a successful trial period.

If you used an agent, you should, as we have already discussed, have agreed to their terms and conditions prior to receiving candidates' details, and in return, the agent, gives you a guarantee. Likewise, they should have already interviewed the candidates they submitted, and checked their references.

An agents' placement invoice is normally sent soon after the candidate has started work, and is required to be paid within a week or two. The fee structure should have been agreed, and there is normally a provision for a reimbursement on a sliding scale, should the candidate not work out.

It is very important to keep a good relationship with any of the agents and candidates you engage with.

This is a very small industry, and many agents know each other and share many of the candidates, with whom very often they have managed for many years.

What you do not want is to gain a bad reputation. This can be from any of the following:

- Not paying the fee, or not paying it on time.
- Haggling the fee after you've signed the terms and conditions.
- Rudeness or being generally disrespectful or unpleasant.
- Changing the job description or details of the position once the candidate has started
- Changing the remuneration package once the candidate has started

Once you have offered the candidate the position, you need to follow up all the points you discussed in the interview in a formal contract.

The contract is a formal agreement of employment and as such should be compiled very carefully. You should print out two copies, one signed by yourself as the employer and one by the new employee, and both parties keep a copy.

Here is a simple draft contract for a live-in housekeeper. You may want to draft a much more detailed contract and it may be wise to ask your lawyer to review it or even draw one up.

Mr. Martin Higgins,
165 Eaton Place,
London, SW1
January 12th, 2019

Private and confidential

Dear Anne,

Further to your interview on Sunday, 6th January, it is my pleasure to offer you the Housekeeper's position at our home at 165, Eaton Place, London.

Contract of Employment: The Terms and Conditions are as follows:

The position will commence on Monday, 14th January, 2019. Please come to the staff entrance at our residence at 9.00am, where you will be met by our house manager, Mr John Jones. He will introduce you to our other staff, arrange your uniform and help you get settled in, and give you a set of keys.

Your salary will be fixed at £35,000 net. This will be payable monthly in arrears by BACS payment into your personal bank account. This will be reviewed after the first three (3) months, then annually thereafter.

You will be required to work a five-day week, but when we are in residence, we expect you to be available to work each day (7 days a week), to a maximum of four (4) calendar months per annum. The extra days worked can be taken in lieu.

You will be given a statutory annual holiday leave, which is 28 days, (5.6 weeks) which includes all public holidays. However; depending on our program you may not be able to take the bank holidays on the actual day. Applications for holidays must be made to us in writing so that we can ensure that they are taken when we are not in residence.

This position offered is 'live-in,' and as such, we pay all services, including council tax and telephone line rental. However, if you wish to use the staff telephone line, all personal calls should be paid for.

When we are not in residence, your normal working hours will be between 09h00 and 17h30

However, when the house is occupied by family or guests, you will be required to commence work at 08h00, and work through until after dinner, or when everyone leaves for the evening and the bathroom services and bedrooms turned down for the evening, with the appropriate rest breaks taken during the day.

When the family is in residence, meals will be provided. At all other times, you will be responsible for providing your own food. Alcohol must not be consumed on the premises.

Smoking is not permitted.

As this is our private residence, guests are not allowed within the apartment.

You are required to wear a uniform at all times which will be provided by us. You are, however, required to supply your own shoes and tights.

Whilst in our employ, you will report to the Butler/House Manager. Should you have any worries or concerns, then please address them to him in the first instance, and if he is unable to help, you should ask him to relay your concern(s) directly to Mr. Higgins.

The first three (3) months of your employment will be probational, during which, if either party wishes to terminate this agreement, one (1) week's notice will be required. After the trial period, one (1) month's notice will be required to terminate this agreement.

In the event of you being unfit or unwell for work, you will be required to notify us immediately and comply with the rules governing statutory sick pay. If you are absent for more than 7 days, you shall be required to provide a doctor's certificate.

In your capacity as a domestic employee, you shall be responsible for the observance of the health and safety procedures and to adopt safe working practices. Should any situation arise, which in your opinion constitutes a danger to yourself or other employees, guests or the general public, then you should inform the Butler/House Manager immediately.

It is very important that you are discreet, honest and dependable at all times.

We enjoy a quiet environment and privacy when at home. Consequently, we expect that any noise is kept to an absolute minimum, and that loud music or talking should not emanate from the staff areas.

If you are in agreement with these Terms and Conditions, I would be grateful if you would sign the declaration at the bottom, and return the completed letter to me. A second copy is enclosed for your retention.

Yours sincerely,

Martin P. Higgins

CHAPTER 9

Motivation!

N ow that the staff are engaged, how do we ensure that both you and your employee(s) get the most from their job and that they have the motivation to stay with you for many years to come?

A good induction to your home and household is certainly a great start!

You can delegate an existing staff member, ideally your house manager/pa to meet them on their first day and go through any paperwork, such as the Employment Contract, House Rules and SOP Manual. They should introduce them to the other staff members and give them a tour of the residence.

They should be advised on certain key points. These can include:

1. How the family should be addressed;
2. Where they can use the bathroom, take their meals, get changed, and so forth;
3. Where they can and cannot have access to;
4. Emergency procedures—what to do in case of an emergency, where the fire escapes and extinguishers are, and the location of the evacuation point
5. They should be promoted to ask as many questions as they like—we NEVER ASSUME!!

I always recommend to any new and existing members of staff to ask as many questions as they can. I promote the smallest and silliest questions, as more often than not, these can be the most important. I never mind someone asking the same question 100 times until they are sure.

Whenever anyone ASSUMES something or PRESUMES that something should be done a certain way without asking or checking first, is a sure way to make the biggest mistakes!

Once you have great staff in place, you need to ensure you provide a good working environment.

This should include the following key points:

1. That you have the right tools for your staff to carry out their duties. Ensure you have sufficient, up-to-date cleaning equipment, relevant cleaning products and good quality appliances in full working order.

2. Sufficient storage areas throughout the residence for cleaning products, appliances, paper goods, and so forth. Easy access to items that are used on a regular basis.

3. You should have a dedicated and appropriate area in your home for your staff to have breaks and eat their meals.

4. You need to provide an area where they can prepare food and beverages.

5. Your staff should have their own bathroom and cloakroom, somewhere where they can change, and store their personal items securely.

Your Privacy. . . .

If you have not employed full-time domestic staff before, acclimating to their presence in your home can take some getting used to. It is a wonderful concept to have people taking care of most household tasks for you, but what many people initially fail to realise is that that there will be a reduction in the level of privacy - that you will need to get used to, and if you want your household staff to succeed, you will need to let go of a certain amount of control and trust them to do their job. Staff will be coming to you for direction, certainly at the beginning, and you will need to understand that a relationship develops with time.

How you give that direction and control the relationship is crucial.

Too familiar and they can take advantage and feel it is okay, and they will be extremely hard to reprimand, or even worse, to dismiss. If you are too distant, there will be no rapport which can make for an uneasy atmosphere in your home. A controlling behaviour will most likely result in them leaving. So what is the perfect balance?

A dear friend of mine employed a housekeeper for several years. She had great difficulty in finding one that she liked, and consequently, made every effort to ensure her happiness and comfort in the position. Unfortunately, the housekeeper in question was given everything she asked for and more, including extra days off, time off, bonuses and so forth. She made every effort to make her friend, so they would sit and chat, have meals together and so forth. It reached a point where she was hardly doing any work, my friend could not bring herself to reprimand her, and to top it all, she found out that she was gossiping about her to her friends when picking up her children from school!

You should adopt a professional relationship, where you show mutual respect for one another and have scheduled meetings. However formal this may sound, it will keep both your staff and your time in check.

However, when it comes to childcare, i.e. nannies and governesses, their role is, by definition, more personal and they will practically become a member of the family. Consequently, you will need to ensure that your staff understand this relationship, as very often, they see them having preferential treatment.

You should ensure that they know when and where your boundaries lie. For example, it is normal practice in private service that other than the Ladies' maid/valet or nanny, no one should be allowed on the bedroom floor until called or the family have dressed and have gone down to breakfast.

If you prefer to have a relaxed and informal relationship, setting boundaries is even more important. Otherwise, there may be a tendency for any of your staff to think it totally okay to call you or enter any room you may be in to ask you things, sometimes the most trivial, at any moment in time. Initially, you may be okay with this, you will find it increasingly difficult to control, and even harder to correct.

Above all else, THE most important thing to ensure a smooth running home is effective communication.

Time and time again, clear instructions are not given. Incomplete information is given and interpretations are made.

For example . . .

You may call to the kitchen and ask the housekeeper: 'Can you bring me some tea, please'

The following scenarios may ensue:

1. The answer is yes, I can! ;)
2. A box of loose leaf tea is brought up
3. She makes a cup of Builder's tea and you always have Earl Grey
4. She makes the tea and spends half an hour finding out where you are
5. The tea is made in a mug and should be in a tea pot
6. The tea arrives in a cup with no saucer, tea spoon, milk, lemon, sweetener or sugar
7. She did not know you have guests so only has tea for one

You can see how, without proper instruction, training or knowledge, the simplest of tasks can be interpreted so differently.

These interpretations are based on whatever pieces of information the staff member may have gleaned and is complimented with how they would have performed, or the standards that their prior employer would have had. In these situations, it is easy to reprimand them for doing the task incorrectly. However, is it really their fault?!?

Of course not! This is where proper training and SOP Manuals play their part.

SOP Manuals

An SOP or 'Standard of Performance' Manual is the 'go to' reference book for how you want your home to be run. It can be as detailed as you please, and be available for all staff for all duties and tasks to be performed. Anything from making a bed, answering the phone and making a tea tray. The more detail you can include, in a simple easy-to-read format the better. Diagrams and photos are a great contribution. You can photograph various table settings to replicate when entertaining, your bathroom products that need to be kept replenished, an order of service, and so on and so forth. More about this later in the book!

How to create effective channels of communication?

Try to nominate one staff member to meet with, who should be responsible to collate any questions or feedback from your other staff. This way, having just one point person will efficiently help manage your time. That staff member can then report back to your other staff members and relay the details relevant to each of them.

Think carefully about your daily or weekly schedule, and work out what time and days would be most convenient for you. A meeting need only last a few minutes!

From the staff point of view, mid mornings and late afternoons would be the most optimal.

You should try to keep notes or an 'aide memoire'

Please check out Chapter 12 for my system on effective home organization and communication!

A morning meeting would be a great time to confirm the day's arrangements and give feedback from questions and requests that may have been posed the day before.

An afternoon meeting would be a great time to give confirmation on the following day's arrangements.

Meetings could be constructed as follows:

1. Priority points—this may be answers you need from them and they need from you ASAP.

2. Your daily rundown—you should confirm your lunch and dinner requirements, including guests, meal timings and menu choices, as well as any other guests or specific requirements for the day or that you know for the next few days.

3. Staff daily rundown—This may include any contractors or service professionals arranged, such as the florist, window cleaner and so forth.

4. Other issues—You should bring up other points you want them to focus on. This could be that you've noticed light bulbs that are blown, that the breakfast tray was not cleared at an appropriate time, that you need certain errands performed and so forth.

5. Allow time for any other points.

Ambiguity is NEVER a good thing. Staff are generally much happier with clear lines of authority and instruction. Staff much prefer being given clear instruction than to rely on guess work.

CHAPTER 10
Instruction/Direction

The 8-step plan to Effective Instruction.

I have developed this system to enable you to deliver clear instruction to your staff to carry out exactly what it is you need to be done, without misunderstanding or confusion and with the most efficient use of your time, which is your most precious commodity.

The 8 steps can be categorized as follows:

I   -   **Intent**

N -   **Nominate**

S   -   **Situate**

T   -   **Transmit**

R -   **Repeat**

U -   **Understand**

C -   **Check**

T   -   **Treat**

INTENT

You need to be clear in your mind as to exactly what it is you need to have done. This could be anything from running to the dry cleaners to pick up your evening gown, to deep cleaning the kitchen cabinets. Whatever it is, you need to be specific as to what you need to have performed.

For example, asking your housekeeper to bring a tea tray to the living room may seem a simple enough task, but she may not know that two guests just arrived and you need tea for three people, nor would she know what tea you prefer. She is left to assume the specifics, which will be based on either your normal habits or their own experiences.

Consequently, you may end up with her entering the room holding an empty silver tray you normally use to offer tea on, to a mug of builders' tea and a digestive. However, if you had explained that you would like a pot of Earl Grey Tea for three people with sliced lemon on the side and a little milk, she should be able to deliver exactly your intent.*

NOMINATE

Make sure you select the right person(s) for the job. You should not ask the housekeeper to clean the kitchen floor, if it is normally the chef's responsibility to do so. You should have a clear understanding of the roles each of your staff have.

You should not ask the chauffer, for example, to pick up your mobile phone you left at your last appointment if they are now the other side of town and you need it ASAP. However, if you call and explain to your PA, she can call your last appointment, confirm that the phone is there and can go pick it up herself.

Having a full understanding of the roles that each of your staff members have is an essential element of being in control of your household. If you do not, and confuse what duties they are responsible for, it will lead to ambiguity and many problems. Good staff are flexible and generally want to please their employer. Consequently, if you ask them to do something, they will try do it to the best of their ability. So asking them to complete a task that is normally the

---

*   I should point out, that this can only be carried out properly after the correct training and/or having effective training manuals in place to refer to. Hence, she would know how to make the tea, what tea service to use, and how to set up the tray and serve it correctly.

responsibility of another team member can produce the following results:

a.   They automatically think that you cannot trust the staff member that is normally responsible for fulfilling that task.

b.   The staff member who normally does that task will start to question his/her ability and feel insecure

c.   As it is not normally their responsibility, you may need to explain in much greater detail

d.   They may not perform the task to the standard you would like as it is new to them

e.   Another extra task adds to their workload and can feel that they are taken advantage of, overloaded and may feel they deserve remuneration.

SITUATE

Make sure you create the right moment and place to give your instruction. This can be as simple as a phone call to your housekeeper to let them know your bedroom is vacated and they can enter and make the bed, to calling the house manager to ask he joins you at a mutually convenient time to run through your list of requirements for the following day/week.

With this in mind, if you were to inform the chef in the afternoon that you will be entertaining ten guests for dinner, then generally there is not enough notice to perform that instruction.

Many times, a request is called out to someone who may be heavily involved or concentrating on something else. You may be in a hurry, remembered that you needed to ask them to do a particular task, so you call out and deliver your message and rush off, without knowing if your request has been heard, let alone understood. The staff member in question may realise too late, turn round thinking they heard you call out and too late . . . you've gone. They are then left in a panic not knowing if you actually did call out, or what it was that you needed to be done.

TRANSMIT

This is how you deliver your message.

How effectively you transmit the message will determine how close to what you desire will be carried out.

The key elements here are:

Precision of content—Make sure your message is clear and simple to understand

Clarity—Speak clearly and use words and language the recipient will understand

Eye contact/focus—ensure both yourself and the recipient are focused on the conversation

Tonality—Speak in a friendly manner, so the message is received in a positive manner

Accountability—In your delivery, make sure the recipient takes ownership of the task and thus is accountable for the outcome

Respectfulness—Always show respect for whomever you are talking to, otherwise they may not necessarily show respect back

REPEAT

It is good practise to ask the recipient to repeat back to you what it is they are meant to do. Many times staff will nod their head and say yes to you, giving assurance that they understood fully what you asked them to do. However, many times this is not the case. Asking them to repeat what you asked them to do back to you is the only way you will know if they fully understood and prevent you from tearing your hair out!!!

UNDERSTAND

If they did not understand, repeat this process once more on the area or areas of your instruction that were not understood and again, ask them to repeat back to you until they fully understand.

CHECK/complete/communicate

Once the task has been completed, you should check that the result is as you had wanted. This can have many variables that may, for whatever reason, be out of their control. However, you should check-in with them that they were able to complete the task, and if there were any complications, find out what they were in order to eliminate them next time.

TRICK or TREAT

It is very important to give feedback once the task is complete. This need not be immediate nor excessive, nor does it need to be positive if the outcome was not to your liking. However, the delivery must be positive and professional, and time be given for the recipient to give feedback, too.

Reprimanding

To effectively manage your staff, as well as being able to give clear and precise instruction, it will include your ability to reprimand when tasks are not carried out to your satisfaction. No one really likes conflict, and many times, for convenience or lack of time, we choose to let things slide and give people the benefit of the doubt. This is all well and good; however, through time, you will become more and more agitated. You will become more distant to whomever it is you fail to approach, and you may even get to a point where you would rather not have them in your household.

You need to feel comfortable and be able to direct your disapproval in a constructive way, without raising your voice, swearing or being overly emotional. Sometimes the best way is to simply say you are very disappointed, this can be sufficient to make your dedicated staff extremely contrite.

So, the following steps are a possible pattern to follow:

1. If you can ask your head of household to reprimand—do so!

2. If not, ask to meet the person in question at a specific time that day

3. Keep it confidential—do not talk to your other staff about the situation

4. Sit them down in a private setting where you cannot be overheard

5. Explain why you have called them in. Tell them that they are a valued employee and are very well liked and respected, however something has occurred that needs to be discussed.

6. Explain what happened, and express your displeasure over what occurred. Remain calm and do not become personal or emotional

7. Allow them to explain their side of the situation and await an apology, if it is forthcoming

8. Thank them for the explanation and again explain why their action was not acceptable

9. Ask them if they think their action was acceptable, and tell them why you think it was not

10. Ask them how we can move forward together to prevent a similar situation from happening again, or how the present dilemma can be resolved amicably

11. Reaffirm their talents and your relationship with them, and forgive them if you accept their apology

12. Close the meeting

13. Closure and Move on! Do not bring this up again, unless the same issue reoccurs.

14. Do not hold a grudge. Once you have sorted it out, carry on as normal as if nothing has happened.

'To understand all, is to forgive all. Create a rapport'

It is not necessary to linger on the point or go over any wrong doing repeatedly. Know that your displeasure has been noted, and that it has most probably affected them more than you may know.

CHAPTER 11

Your relationship and maintaining your Privacy

If you have engaged great staff for your needs and followed the plan, then your staff should be immensely loyal and strive to please and do their best for you. However, you need to be aware that 'everything comes from the top!' So how you treat your staff and behave can have a direct effect on them. Any small gesture on your part, however slight, can be construed in so many ways and can easily make or break that person's day.

For example, if one day you give a withering look to your enthusiastic housekeeper who just put down your breakfast tray and who is normally given a 'thank you' and a smile (perhaps you just discovered you had arranged to meet someone for lunch that you'd rather not). She may construe that as having done something to displease you, she may then spend the rest of the day anxious to know what it was she did wrong and thus not perform to her best.

It is human nature to make 1 and 1 = 5. We all make assumptions, which most of the time are completely wrong! We generally tend to think that we have done something wrong, if the other party seems unhappy or upset in our presence and has not communicated a reason why. More often than not, we think up so many reasons how we could have upset someone and create entire scenarios in our heads if a normal pattern of behaviour has been disrupted.

This also brings us to the point of ensuring, as an employer, you always follow through with whatever you have discussed or promised. . . .

KEEP YOUR PROMISES!

First name versus Mr, Mrs or Madam/Ma'am?

It is important that you decide how you would like your staff to address you and your family members.

A PA or nanny would normally address you and your family by your first name; though this is certainly not written in stone.

I would highly recommend that to keep things on a professional level, you are addressed by your title, ie Mr or Mrs Smith, and your children, whatever age, by their first names. You must be consistent though.

Outward signs of affection

Keeping things on a professional level can still give you the occasion to give the occasional hug or kiss on the cheek if you so wish; once you have established a relationship and a comfort level with your staff. This may be appropriate on the occasion of their birthday, Christmas, or perhaps if you are leaving on an extended trip or returning from one, give them a hug or a kiss on both cheeks; it is a lovely gesture and cements a level of mutual affection and reaffirms that they are appreciated and will be or have been missed. Prior to establishing this rapport, which may take a while, a handshake is equally appreciated, especially between men.

Acknowledge their Birthdays

A really nice way to show your gratitude and appreciation would be to recognise your employees' birthdays each year. Again, consistency is paramount—all staff, every year! This may well be in the form of a monetary bonus. Asking your chef to bake a cake or purchasing one is also a lovely idea, and this way, all your staff can benefit!

Formal, Informal or Casual

You need to decide on how you would like your home to run. A formally run home doesn't necessarily mean that it will be akin to Downtown Abbey! To have structure, and an environment where everyone has all the information they need at hand, where everyone knows what to do and how and when to do it, to work together and give you the level of privacy you require can be achievable whether you prefer formality or a casually run home.

Keeping Consistency

It is important for staff morale that you keep consistency with all your staff at all times. You should not show favouritism, as this can lead to jealousy and staff competing for your attention, and can even lead to staff withholding information from each other or setting each other up to fail.

One employer explained to me the reason she seldom acknowledged anyone in the morning. It was always thought that she was aloof or simply ignored her staff. It was really not the case. If she were to stop and say good morning to one staff member, she would have to say good morning to each one of us every day. And with a household of nine, she would lose whatever train of thought she had and not be able to concentrate on the business of the day. She is quite right. It is similar to the morning commute—you may get the same train every day and see the same faces.

Do you say hi and start a conversation? Generally not, as you know that if you see them the next day, and the day after that, and so forth, you will need to acknowledge them every time or they will think something is wrong, or you may even end up catching an earlier train to avoid them!

Hierarchy

There is a general hierarchy in the staff 'pecking order!' However archaic this may sound, it is still very much valid. Everyone should have their specific duties to perform but still have the flexibility to help each other, and cover other staff if they're busy, off duty, sick or on vacation. You do not want the 'not my job' attitude.

Key communicators in your household

If you plan on having a number of staff in your home, to prevent being emailed, messaged and called by everyone, whenever they wish, set up a chain of command. So you only receive emails or calls from the key person or persons.

Your staff need to understand the hierarchy in your home. Knowing they can come to you in an emergency or personal crisis is one thing, but you need to establish a chain of command, so they know who to ask for direction and assistance and not come to you constantly.

Maintaining your privacy

Having a staffed home can easily result in a lack of privacy. So setting up a few rules of when you do not want to be disturbed is crucial.

Your staff need to know where and when you need your privacy and when not to disturb you. This is entirely up to you, but it is generally accepted that staff, other than perhaps the valet or ladies' maid, should not be on the bedroom floor prior to the family coming downstairs, unless delivering a breakfast tray.

It is also customary for staff to only knock on bedroom doors before entering. All other rooms (bathrooms excluded of course) unless otherwise mentioned, staff can access freely.

Therefore, make it clear that if a door is closed, that means you need your privacy unless of an emergency.

You may want to suggest your preferred forms of communication. Do you prefer that questions are submitted to you via email or SMS/WhatsApp rather than through the phone system, so that you can answer in YOUR time and not theirs.

Would you like staff to send you reminders if you haven't answered them on time sensitive matters?

Privacy works both ways, so your staff will need their own area too, where they know they will not be disturbed on breaks too, especially if they are working long hours.

Your household staff are in fact, another family co-existing in the same house.

I recall one comment, years ago, that criticised HM The Queen, for never visiting her own kitchen at Buckingham Palace. Well, she is quite right! Being who she is, how would you, as a chef in a busy kitchen, be able to concentrate, if you knew The Sovereign could come along at any given moment!—You would be a nervous wreck! Of course, I'm not saying you should NEVER visit the staff areas, but it is just as important for them to have their privacy, as it is for you as the employer, to have yours. Even if it is just to put their feet up and wind down for 10 minutes or to even have a private 'scream' moment, if things are getting stressful!— It will!!

SOPs or 'Standard of Performance Manuals'

As I discussed, you should put together a comprehensive Standard of Performance Manual, so every member of your household has the information they need to carry out your wishes. This should include points relating to timings and scheduling. For example . . .

It is actually only customary for staff to knock on bedroom doors before entering. Otherwise, it is generally acknowledged that they can open the door to any reception room or office and enter.

Your staff should know to vacate a room you have entered, quietly and quickly, unless instructed to the contrary, without questioning.

You need to ensure the cleaning schedule is co-ordinated with your daily routine. If you tend not to use the reception rooms until late morning, then they should be cleaned in the morning. Once you have vacated your bedroom and bathroom, then the bed can be made and bathroom cleaned and so on and so forth.

You should also include in your Performance Manual a standard time to work to when clearing tea/coffee trays, drawing the curtains, asking you if you require anything, and so on and so forth. This way you will know when to expect a visit.

For example, you could set a standard to request your staff to return to remove a tea tray 20 minutes after it was brought in.

Then ask that curtains be drawn and lighting levels adjusted (again to your preference!) but normally it is once you can see your reflection in the windows.

In the software program we have created to aid the organisation of homes, there is a section for **standard of performance manuals** for any operation, table setting or procedure you would wish; that can be for anything from how to iron embroidered table linen to how to serve at a formal dinner. It can be adapted to any number of tasks you wish!

Try.housemartin.app

House Rules

To accompany your Employees Contract and the Standard of Performance Manual, you should compile a short, yet comprehensive list of house rules or 'Rules of Conduct'. This should set the tone of how you like your home to be run, and what level of behaviour and conduct you deem unacceptable.

Having experienced various issues with staff over the years, I know what needs to be included to prevent dramas becoming a crisis.

Here is a copy of some rules I drew up for a client who had just set up a new household:

RULES OF CONDUCT

- The Principles require that their home be a quiet and peaceful place at all times. They want a harmonious environment. Therefore, you must always conduct yourself in a professional and dignified manner whilst at work, and leave any personal problems at home.

- Flexibility is paramount. There may be times when you are asked to work late, or it may not be possible to take a break, or have to work over the weekend or on days off, or assist in other properties overseas. Time will always be given to compensate this and your flexibility will be valued greatly.

- When guests are present enter occupied rooms for service purposes only.

- Interpersonal staff communication should be professional, mature and courteous in nature.

- Discussion of anything having to do with the Principles' Family outside of the workplace is prohibited.

- The discussion of individual salaries and bonuses is prohibited among staff members and is cause for dismissal.

- Uniforms are to be worn at all times and are to be clean, pressed and fresh.

- Be prompt to work and call with an explanation if you are going to be late.

- If you have any sign of a cold or flu or any other contagious illness, especially when The Principles are in residence, please inform them ASAP and refrain from coming into work until you are no longer infectious.

- Please refrain from wearing heavily scented perfumes or inappropriate make-up. Women are requested to wear their hair in a ponytail or bun whenever possible.

- Chewing gum is prohibited.

- Smoking is prohibited.

- Drug taking is a case for instant dismissal.

- Consumption of alcoholic beverages is prohibited.

- Staff areas are to be kept clean, tidy and organised.

- Guests are not allowed to be brought onto the property.

- Staff meals are to be taken in the staff areas. Meals will be provided for staff when the family and/or guests are in residence. Something to eat in the evening will also be provided if staff work past 8pm. If you require extra food or prefer to eat something other than provided, then this will be at your expense and you should not take time out or make a separate trip for this.

- The Swimming Pool and garden areas are out of bounds for staff use.

- Staff mobile phones are to be kept on vibrate and used during staff meal times or breaks. Texting is also confined to staff meal times and breaks. Work related calls and messages are exempt, but should be kept to a minimum when the family are in residence and be as discrete as possible.

- Please ensure the main line telephone is answered within three rings.

- When answering the phone say "Good morning/afternoon/evening (name) speaking".

- PHONE MESSAGES: should be accurate and legible. Write the time of call, name, any message and phone number. ALWAYS REPEAT information taken. Write your name as the message taker. Bring phone messages to the recipient immediately or leave them in the pre-approved place for them to see upon their return.

- When answering the door intercom say, "Hello, may I help you?" Only open the door once you know who it is, or if a delivery is for a named person.

- Never leave the property unoccupied with windows or doors open and unlocked with the alarm switched off, even if you are returning within a few minutes.

- The Principles want their home to be GREEN. Therefore, turn off lights in rooms that are not in use and strive to use as many ecologically sound products as possible; confirm before making large purchases.

- The last person to leave at night should see that all doors and windows are locked unless the Principles require certain windows left open if they are in residence. Please check with them each evening.

- Please always try and discuss any inter staff problems as soon as they crop up. Communicating with each other should always be the first step, and is generally the key to resolving any issues quickly and effectively before they become a more serious issue.

- All QUESTIONS are encouraged and welcomed. This is the only way to get things carried out correctly. Please direct questions to the House Manager.

- Please report any problems, breakages and faults as soon as they arise.
- I have read and agree to all the points listed above.

_____

PRINT NAME

_____

SIGNATURE

_____

DATE

CHAPTER 12

Welcome to Calm!

I sincerely hope that the passages I have put together will give you some insight into the how best to navigate the World of domestic staff. It is one of the oldest industries in The World, and there are now more people employed in the domestic service industry, than in any other time in history.

If you only use this as a guide to refer to when engaging staff or resolving issues, it will be of great value.

From my experience working in some incredible residences alongside exceptional staff, the same problems always cropped up.

These generally were a result of bad communication, a lack of clarity, instruction and no effective organizational systems in place. The simplest of requests had the propensity to cause a multitude of dilemmas.

I have put a lot of thought into how these same issues could be prevented and why it was that they were always repeated time and time again in most every household? There was nothing that I could find, that existed to help solve these issues.

Consequently, over the last couple of years, I have teamed up with my good friend Erin Woodger and his business Woodger Limited. Together we have created software to assist in the organisation of fine homes and the running and synchronisation for employers with multiple homes around The World.

This system has been devised to be very easily used by both the Family and staff members to effectively run the residences with the ability to share only required information to relevant parties.

Try.housemartin.app

Erin Woodger grew up in the North of England; his Grandfather worked with Alan Turrin and helped create the World's first computer. On seeing this ground breaking machine as a child at the National Science Museum Erin was inspired by his heritage and has built on that history ever since.

Spending years as a fine cabinet maker and Antique restorer he built computer systems and developed processes to run the various business he was part of.

In 2016 he set up Woodger Limited with his younger brother Gabriel and partner Naomi Brown. Together they have built unique software in various industries, all developed from their passion for taking complicated structures and processes and crafting easy to use solutions that bring simplicity to the user whilst taking care of all the hard work seamlessly in the background.

The house management system will be available in a ready to go format, as well as in individual modules, and there is the option to create a bespoke model to be able to accommodate and control existing software and systems that you may currently have in place in any of your homes around The World.

Here are a few examples of how it can help streamline your homes . . .

For example, you or any named staff member can be alerted wherever you or they are if, for example, you're AC units break down in your New York apartment.

You can choose from a range of modules; such as the inventory section, menus, infinite calendars that can be viewed together or separated to be able to see how your itinerary and schedule overlaps with that of your family and staff and so forth.

We have ensured that the PA and staff members can easily input relevant information. Anything from family and guest details, art, furniture or wine inventories (with the ability to easily contact our wine distributor, at a click of a button to reorder if stocks are depleted anywhere in the World at the most competitive price).

As the Principle, you will be able to easily and simply view all the details and make changes or edits at will. Any changes you make can, if you so wish be instantly messaged to any relevant party. For example, if you make last minute changes to your itinerary, then an alert can be sent to both your driver and pa.

Your housekeeper and other staff members can easily access just the details relevant to them without having to contact yourself, or be bamboozled with a constant stream of text messages/updates that may not be relevant to them.

All your information will be 100% secure, and you will no longer be dependent on the most efficient staff to run your life and residences. Any staff changes in your household will be much smoother, as all the relevant information will be at hand for new employees to access.

If I can be of any further assistance to you through my products and services, I would be deeply honoured to serve you once again.

I look forward to meeting you and hearing about your successes in person. Until then, may I wish you all the health, wealth and happiness in the World!

For further advice and to discuss your particular needs, meet Martin at Martin@housemartinoflondon.com

Try.housemartin.app

Printed in Poland
by Amazon Fulfillment
Poland Sp. z o.o., Wrocław

64326905R00078